CELEBRATE THE DAY

A Collection of Inspirational Poetry and Reflections

HEALEY E. IKERD

Celebrate the Day

Printed in the United States of America

Dedication

To my son, Dedrick,
whose presence in my life helps me understand God's love and grace.

Title	Page

Title	Page

Preface

Most of this book has been on the shelf waiting to be put together for over 20 years. To finally have it published is a great accomplishment!

God has used writing and especially poetry to help me express feelings and thoughts when it has been hard to express them in any other way.

The photographs are my own and are an expression of what I see as beautiful. They remind me of how much God loves us in that he would create such an awesome place to live.

Beauty is indeed all around us, showing us the true splendor of the Lord. I hope you can experience that through these humble words and photographs.

May God bless you as you enjoy all his wonderful gifts in life!

To God be the glory!

Healey

For since the creation of the world God's invisible qualities—his eternal power and divine nature—have been clearly seen, being understood from what has been made, so that people are without excuse.
Romans 1:20

That is why, for Christ's sake, I delight in weaknesses, in insults, in hardships, in persecutions,
in difficulties. For when I am weak, then I am strong.
2 Corinthians 12:10

THE PATH OF LIFE

TO BRING GLORY TO THE ALMIGHTY GOD,
IT IS HIS ROAD, I WILL TAKE.
FOR ON HIS PATH ARE TRUTH AND LIGHT,
OH, WHAT A DIFFERENCE HE DOES MAKE.

THE PATHS MAY BE UNFAMILIAR,
BUT ON EACH ONE GOD DOES GUIDE,
TO THE PLACE HE HAS PREPARED,
AS LONG AS IN HIM WE ABIDE.

HE GIVES US THE POWER TO WALK
FOR ON THIS PATH, HE IS OUR FEET.
WE TAKE THE TRAIL OF VICTORY,
FOR ON IT, WE KNOW NO DEFEAT.

THE GREATEST OF HIS POWER,
THE AWESOMENESS OF HIS GRACE,
HAVE A GREAT TUGGING AT OUR SOUL,
AS WE TRAVEL TO SEE HIS FACE.

HE GUIDES US AND LEADS US,
SO THAT WE WILL NOT GO ASTRAY.
BUT IF WE DO, HIS LOVE IS TRUE,
FOR IT WAS FOR OUR LIVES HIS SON DID LAY.

OH GOD, YOU ARE MY GOD,
MAY I BRING THE GLORY YOU ARE DUE.
FOR I WAS LAME AND YOU HELPED ME WALK,
ON THE PATH THAT LEADS TO YOU.

When will I know..?

It hurts...

It hurts deep down in my soul,

It hurts further than a knife could ever go.

I have prayed for so many years.

And now...

I don't know.

Did you answer my prayers?

Will I ever know?

Will you tell me here or will you wait...?

It hurts...

It hurts not knowing...unsure of the verdict.

I have to trust in you. I have to believe.

For I know that you love

much greater than I ever could.

I know you hurt

much deeper than I ever will.

Yet...will I know?

THE SON

He wasn't just any Son.

He was the Son.

He was the Son sent for me from the Father.

Through this Son would be how I would come to know the Father.

That is why He sent His Son.

His Son was no ordinary man.

He was the Light and the Truth.

And He became flesh for me.

He lived his life perfect for me. So that I would know how to live.

Then He was killed. Killed by the very people who praised Him weeks earlier.

He wasn't who they expected. He claimed to be God, of God.

They didn't understand.

The Son was nailed to a cross between two criminals.

He was humiliated, spit at, jeered at, and taunted.

A Man who lived without sin.

He experienced things many of us fear.

He knew it was necessary.

The Son was nailed to the cross.

While He hung he carried something on His back.

It weighed more than any pound known.

On His back were the sins of this world.

My sins. Your sins. My sins alone were heavy.

I weep to think of His pain.

I think, "Why would he put himself through this for me? For any of us?

I don't deserve it."

I hear His words through the darkness, "because I love you."

He gave me the most wonderful gift ever given.

The gift of God's only Son, Jesus, who is now alive.

Alive in the world and alive in me.

All because He loves me.

Only You

God, You are all I need to be complete.

You are what I need when I feel

Alone.

Sad.

Unloved.

Hungry.

Scared.

Ugly.

Lost.

Tired.

Cold.

Only You, my Father in Heaven,

can cleanse me

and

fill me

until I am whole once more.

Thank you, Father, for healing me

Every day of my life.

Jesus answered, "I am the way and the truth and the life.
No one come to the Father except through me."
John 14:6

For where two or three are gathered in my name, there am I among them." Matthew 18:20

An Awesome Master

O God,

You are awesome.

Never have I had a Master who

gives so much to me.

You gave love to me

when I didn't want it.

You gave forgiveness to me

even though I didn't deserve it.

God, You give things of gold to me.

All the days of my life.

You are so faithful, Father.

God, I know I can never repay You for all that You have done for me.

So, in this moment, Lord God, I give You all I have, all that I am.

I give you my life.

God, You know at times I may ask for it back.

I may even demand it back.

Father,

please don't listen to me in those times.

I know that You can do more with my life than I could ever desire.

Take my life, O God, and do with it as You please.

I am Your servant.

I want to make You, my Master, pleased with what I do.

I cannot do that though without Your help.

Guide me and keep me O God.

And thank you for allowing me to be a servant of You, the Almighty.

In Your Son's name.

Amen.

Peace

Our minds reach out

Trying to comprehend

Trying to make sense

Not sure why...when....how..

why....WHY???...

So many questions,

No easy answers

Your hand is there

Ready to give strength and comfort

Though still not revealing answers.

It's not time to understand.

To ponder, to see.

Not today.

Today is a day for trust

Without knowing why,

Or understanding,

But finding peace just the same.

Unproclaimed Good News

Jesus whispers to me in my ear,
"I love you".
I must proclaim from the rooftops what I know!

Why don't I.....?

The Lord God tells me in the dark,
"I have forgiven you."
I must shout this message from the hilltops in the light of day!

But I don't....

God sent his only son to die for me, so that I could one day join Him in
His kingdom.
A place more wonderful than the imagination can create.
A place where we will see
and be in the presence of the Lord God Almighty,
the Creator of Heaven and Earth!
I must climb the highest mountain
until everyone hears the Good News:
Jesus is Alive!!!

So why don't I......?

Jesus told me to speak in the daylight what He tells me in the dark and to
proclaim from the rooftops what He whispers in my ear.
I cannot be afraid.
I must remember what God has promised me.
I must remember He loves me.
To show I love Him, I have to do what He asks.

Unexpected

All alone, he walks in
Not a tear on his face
How far he had come,
No longer a stranger to this place.

He had a good job,
A dog brown and black
Good friends and a car.
Now, no way to go back.

Nowhere to move my eyes
As he steps through the line
My glance catches his
And it's love that I find.

He asks how I am
and then blesses my day
I am humbled that God
Would bless me this way.

Who am I to think
That only I can share
God's blessings of kindness,
Compassion, and care.

Though hungry and dirty
nowhere to go at night.
We are all God's children
Only different battles to fight.

When Jesus spoke again to the people, he said, "I am the light of the world. Whoever follows me will never walk in darkness, but will have the light of life." John 8:12

Oh, how I love your law! I meditate on it all day long.

Psalm 119:97

The Way

Fear will not reign in me,
Evil will not thrive.
For it is by the Word I live
And it is in God that I survive

I know not fear; but only the Way
He is the one who set me free.
I know not desperation like I once knew,
Only the Life which lives inside of me.

The Truth sets me free,
From the chains that once bound.
Jesus is the way and truth,
It is in him that I have been found.

I know not death,
For it is life God has given to me.
He grants me all I need,
To live in peace and victory.

What He Gave

Light is what He gave when I lived in darkness.
Truth is what He gave when I lived a lie.
Help is what He gave when I called.

He forgives when I sin.
He strengthens when I am weak.
He provides when I am lost.

Faith is what He gave when I gave up.
A hand is what He gave when I fell.
Hope is what he gave when I was unsure.

He Comforts when I am sad.
He Loves when I am alone.
He Builds what I lack.

Sacrifice is what He gave me before I knew who He was.

Oh, what gifts He gives!!
How blessed am I!!!
May I give all that he has freely given me!!!

My Mother

My mother, you cared for me before I could speak.

You taught me those first steps.

My mother, you taught me to brush my teeth and say my prayers.

You fed me when I was hungry

and gave me water when I was thirsty.

Behind each lesson you taught and behind each meal you made

was your unbinding love for me.

Now I am grown, my mother and you still give and you still teach.

And your love is still unbound.

And although I know how to walk, you still teach me how to get up again.

And because of your lessons of brushing teeth and saying prayers

is why I, now, know discipline

and I, now, know God.

You still feed me if I am hungry and

you still give me water if I thirst.

I thank you for those things and

I thank you, especially for your love that knows no bounds.

Now, I am a mother also.

I have to teach my child those same things.

I thank you, my mother, for the lessons.

And I thank God, for making you my teacher.

The Search

It began as you saw them leave
And continued as you grew up.
It's been long and painful
Like the filling of a broken cup.

You've been tattered and torn
By those intended to love you most.
You wish you could go back
To the time there were no ghosts.

It is darkness that resides in you
How do you now live?
What they have done...there is no going back.
What do you have left to give?

It was then that you heard him,
a quiet whisper only you could hear.
"Come to me. I will heal," He said.
As he wiped away a tear.

"At least there is hope for a tree: If it is cut down, it will sprout again, and its new shoots will not fail. Its roots may grow old in the ground and its stump die in the soil, yet at the scent of water it will bud and put forth shoots like a plant."   Job 14:7-9

The heavens declare the glory of God; the skies proclaim the work of his hands. Psalm 19:1

Who Am I?

Who am I?
I am nothing without Jesus.
I can bear no fruit without Him.
I might as well be thrown away
like a dead branch if I am without Him.

Who am I?
I am a person who sins.
I want to be good...still I sin.
I want to be fruitful...still I sin.

Who am I?
I am one of millions
who loaded the back of Jesus with my sin.
He bore it all.
He took on what I could not.
He is strong because I am not.

Who am I?
I am someone God has made and called.
I am someone that God has forgiven.
I am someone that God loves.

Who am I?
I am a mother.
I am someone God trusted with one of his own children.
I am part of His family.

Who am I?
I am someone that God loves.
I am someone that Jesus loves.
The Holy Spirit dwells within me.

Who am I?
I am someone who is not of this world.
I have another home because I have believed.
I have a Father waiting there for me.

Who am I?
I am someone that is not always deserving of blessings.
I am not always sinless.
I am not always faithful.

Who am I?
I am someone loved by the Creator of heaven and earth.
I am someone forgiven by the Father of Compassion.
I am someone comforted by the Lord God Almighty.

Who am I?
I am not someone that this world deems important.
However, I am important to someone.
I am important to God.
And He made me his child.

Who am I?
I am exactly who God has made me to be.

Long Awaited

The promise of one day.

One day that has been long awaited.

HE knew it would come.

As many doubted,

many hoped.

Two believed.

A day long awaited,

for a day of a new journey.

A journey of several roads

but now only one together.

It has been long awaited

and sometimes tangled along the way.

It is here.

May God bless this new road together.

My Father

You have been my Father,
when my family wasn't there.
You have been my Father,
when my friends did not care.

You have been my Father
long before I even knew,
You listened when I spoke,
and watched me as I grew.

Today, You are still my Father true,
even though I am grown.
I love You with all that I am.
Though still like a field, just newly sown.

Father, I love you more.
More than any friend or family.
You are helping me become the person,
the person I am called to be.

You're making me a person of worth.
Because I love You with all my mind,
I can be a friend, a mother or a sister.
Father, my heart and soul are thine.

Father, 'tis an honor to be called.
Called to do what You ask.
An honor is it to be Your child,
Enable me, God, to complete the task.

Saying Goodbye

It's hard to say good-bye,

to let it all go.

It holds my tears of both joy and sadness.

In it lies long days of toil

and days of loneliness.

It holds my weaknesses made strong.

It holds my ignorance made wise.

It is hard to say goodbye,

to let it all go.

Will it remain the same?

Or be better? Or worse?

Can I know? Will they forget?

Who I was? My labor of love?

It is hard to say goodbye,

To let it all go.

It seems like it holds it all,

but it doesn't.

It was You.

"My grace is sufficient for you, for my power is made perfect in weakness."
2 Corithians 10:9

He is the Rock, his works are perfect, and all his ways are just.
A faithful God who does no wrong, upright and just is he. Deuteronomy 32:4

He is All

Praise to the **Lord**, our **Maker**.
Praise to the **Faithful God**, who does no wrong.
Praise to the **Holy One**.
Praise to the **Creator** of the heavenly lights.
Praise to the **Yahweh**.
Praise to the **Rock** in whom I take refuge.
Praise to **God Most High**.
Praise to the compassionate and **gracious God**.
Praise to the **Shephard** of his people.
Praise to the great **I AM**.
Praise to the **Father** of the fatherless.
Praise to the eternal **King**.
Praise to the **Judge** of all the earth.
Praise to **El Shaddai**.
Praise to **He who blots out your transgressions**.
Praise to the **Redeemer**.
Praise to the **Rock of our salvation**.
Praise to the **King of Glory**.
Praise to the **One who sustains** me.
Praise to the **God of Truth**.
Praise to the **Spring of Living Water**.
Praise to the **El Roi**.
Praise to the **Shelter** in the storm.
Praise to the **Lord God Almighty**,
For **He is all**!!

My Teacher

God, You have entrusted me, with a most precious child.

You knew that I needed to learn some things that You can only teach

through a child.

You gave me my son,

to help me understand how great is Your love for me.

You gave me my son to draw me closer to You.

You gave me my son

to teach me patience and understanding.

You gave me my son

so that I would understand about discipline and love.

God, I have learned lessons that I would have otherwise lost.

God, this child is more than gift,

he is my growth in You.

He is a promise of the future.

He is Your child.

You have entrusted him to me, so that You could teach me.

You gave me my son

and taught me about unconditional love, kindness, grace, and mercy.

You taught me about hope, faith and joy.

God, You gave me my son and I love him with all that I am.

I know You love him even more. I am thankful that You do.

God, I know I have many more lessons to learn.

I thank You that You chose this child to teach me.

A Moment

There was a moment, my God, I asked You to love me.

You took me in Your arms and held me tight.

There was a moment, Father, I asked You to forgive me.

Your mercy overwhelmed my soul.

There was a moment, Lord, I asked You for a gift.

Out of love, you gave the gift of Your only Son.

There was a moment, my Maker, I asked for the Light.

Now I can see, for You are the Light.

There was a moment, Master, I worshipped from my knees.

For I am humbled by Your awesome grace.

Oh God, My Father in Heaven,

Each moment that I breathe,

Let me breathe that moment for You.

Prayer Unanswered

Ask and it will be given…
For everyone who asks, receives, you say,
How long and how much should I ask?
When will you answer? What hour? What day?

Ten years have passed since I first asked.
Why is it not me, this gift to receive?
Is my sin too great? Did I tarry too long?
Is there a hidden treasure I have yet to grieve?

The questions why I often wonder,
I do my best to be strong.
I have done all that I know,
Yet I still wonder why so long.

I will pray longer if I must,
But if I am hindering, let me know.
I will do whatever you ask,
Tell me where and I will go.

I know your promises are true.
No matter what they say.
Whatever it takes, wherever I go,
I will wait in prayer, day by day.

"I tell you," he replied, "if they keep quiet, the stones will cry out." Luke 19:40

From that time on Jesus began to preach, "Repent, for the kingdom of heaven has come near."
Matthew 4:17

With Me

With Me, you will feel love like you have never felt before.

With Me, you will see all that you were once blind to.

With Me, you will know what it means to be My child.

With Me, you will have the peace I promised you.

With Me, you will be comforted in times of sorrow.

With Me, you will never be alone.

With Me, you will be given gifts that you would otherwise

not receive.

With Me, you will be given a new life that extends beyond

this one.

With Me, the yoke is easy and the burden is light.

Why would you want to be anywhere else,

but with Me?

So do not fear, for I am with you; do not be dismayed, for I am your God.
I will strengthen you and help you; I will uphold you with my righteous right hand.
Isaiah 41:10

For God so loved the world that he gave his one and only Son, that whoever believes in him shall not perish but have eternal life. John 3:16

A Prayer

God the Father,

I pray a prayer for this world.

That we, as a nation of Christians, become one for You.

That we become lights of You.

God,

I pray a prayer for this world.

That we, as a nation of Christians, learn to love.

That we love all people who are the same as well as those who differ.

Oh God,

I pray a prayer for this world.

That we, as a nation of Christians,

are courageous in who we believe You to be.

That we are able to tell what we know in truth and in love.

Father,

I pray a prayer for this world.

That we, as a nation of Christians,

stand up and stand firm for who we are, Your children.

That we act like Your children, doing what you want us to do.

Working like you want us to work.

A Prayer
Cont.

Lord God,

I pray a prayer for this world.

That we, as a nation of Christians, can unite.

For a house divided against itself cannot stand.

We want to be the people You call us to be.

Oh wonderful God,

I pray a prayer for this world.

That we, as a nation of Christians, be who we say we are.

Believers in Christ.

For if we believe, then we obey.

For if we obey, then we love.

We want to love You and love others, like You have called us to do.

Oh, Glorious God,

I have a prayer for this world.

That we, as a nation of Christians, do not become like this world.

That we recognize there is but one world that we belong.

Help us to change this world without becoming like it.

A Prayer

Cont.

Oh, Compassionate God,

I know that we, as a nation of Christians,

have let walls be built between us.

We have forgot the prayer that Jesus prayed for us.

That we be brought to complete unity

so that the world would know that You sent Him

and that You loved us even as You loved Him.

Oh, God,

I pray a prayer for this world.

That Your will be done, God.

That we, as a nation of Christians, do Your will.

Help us to do that.

Help us to follow You regardless of the cost,

for we know our reward will be great in Heaven above.

Fill us with Your love, God, so that we can share that love with this world.

Merciful and faithful God,

Thank you.

For I know through You, we can do all things.

Always There

Although I fall,
He is always there to pick me up.

Although I stray,
He is always there to look for me.

Although I get busy,
He always has the time.

Although I forget,
He always reminds me that He loves me.

He is always there for me.
I should always be there for Him.

A Young Girl's Dream

As a young girl growing up,
I often dreamed of the perfect man.
Setting standards they must meet,
and hoping that they can.

It is the love I have dreamed of
my whole life through.
And when it finally happened,
I couldn't believe it was true.

It was out of the blue,
that the perfect man walked.
He was strong and gentle
and spoke of wisdom when he talked.

He told me he loved me,
Not for my past or what I have done.
His love is a true love.
Without it, I am like the earth without a sun.

No one can fill me like he does,
No one can even compare.
Oh God, thank you for this man,
It is for me that he cares.

This man teaches me how to live.
He is what I strive to be.
Without him, I am lost.
But when I call, he is all I see.

His name is Jesus.
He is the perfect man.
Sent from God to the earth.
With him forever, I will stand.

He is a man, the perfect man.
He is my savior true.
He saved me from all my sins.
Yes, he can be your man too!!

Then you will call on me and come and pray to me, and I will listen to you.
You will seek me and find me when you seek me with all your heart.
Jeremiah 29:12-13

When you pass through the waters, I will be with you; and when you pass through the rivers, they will not sweep over you. When you walk through the fire, you will not be burned; the flames will not set you ablaze. Isaiah 43:2

ANOTHER PLACE PREPARED FOR ME

YES, IT IS TRUE.

I AM NOT OF THIS WORLD.

I AM A FOREIGNER.

YES, I DO LOOK LIKE EVERYONE ELSE HERE,

BUT THIS PLACE IS NOT MY HOME.

I AM FROM ANOTHER PLACE.

AND I WILL SOON BE GOING BACK.

I AM JUST HERE VISITING,

TRYING TO DEEPEN MY RELATIONSHIP WITH GOD.

DO YOU WONDER WHERE I AM FROM?

I HAVE TO TELL YOU THE TRUTH.

I COME FROM A PLACE WHERE

THE LAME WALK,

THE BLIND SEE,

THE DEAF HEAR,

THE MUTE SPEAK,

THE SICK ARE HEALED,

THE POOR ARE RICH,

THE WEAK ARE STRONG

AND THE SAD ARE JOYFUL.

MY HOME IS WITH THE MAKER OF HEAVEN AND EARTH.

YES, I WILL LIVE WITH THE LORD GOD ALMIGHTY.

IT IS TRUE.

I AM NOT OF THIS WORLD.

AND I TRULY CAN'T WAIT TO GET HOME.

An Important Life

You were only a few weeks old
but very valuable and very loved.
Though you still had a long time to
grow and develop,
we anxiously,
hopefully,
and joyfully,
thought about your arrival.

You were created by God's own hands,
In his own image
And placed in my womb.
And though you are no longer there,
We are comforted
That God now holds you
Again in His hands.
He holds our hands
As we miss you and
Realize how thankful we are
For what you brought us,
Joy Alive,
Faith Sustained,
Hope Renewed,
And Love Embraced.

We look forward to the day
We are able see you and
To hold you in our arms.

Be Not

Be not afraid;
For it is courage to you I give.
The courage to love and to care
I grant you the courage to live.

Be not downhearted;
For it is joy I give to you.
To help you laugh and play.
I grant it in all you do.

Be not alone;
For I send to you my son.
He loves you as much as I.
His life he has given for everyone.

Be not silent;
For I give to you my Word;
Through the spirit your mouth may speak
That the Truth may be heard throughout the world.

Be not weak;
For what I give will make you strong.
The strength to stand, the strength to fight;
when all is against you and says you are wrong.

Be not bound;
From bondage, you have been set free
Live as if you are unbound,
Live as I have called you to be.

Beautiful Are We

As the beauty in each thing you have created is different,

so is the beauty within each of us.

Beautiful is the grandeur of a mountain tucked in the clouds.

Just as beautiful are the colors of our skin.

Beautiful is the ocean water as it splashes alive on the beach.

Just as beautiful are the strange words that come from our mouths.

As your created world of beauty differs, God,

so do we, your created people.

Each of your creations possess a beauty,

And each beauty is truly unique.

The same with each person you have created, Lord.

Each has beauty and yet, each is different.

And even though, the beauty in each is not the same,

the beauty always exists.

As we appreciate the glory of the world you have created

and such beautiful things in it,

help us remember that we too, are created.

And we too, are beautiful.

We aren't all seas, and we aren't all mountains.

But we are all made beautiful in what you have called us to be.

As the beauty in each thing you have created is different,

so is the beauty within each of us.

The Lord your God is with you, the Mighty Warrior who saves.
He will take great delight in you; in his love he will no longer rebuke you,
but will rejoice over you with singing." Zephaniah 3:17

God has said, "Never will I leave you; never will I forsake you.
Hebrews 13:5

Can I Be a Blessing?

A day.
A smile gives little to change what they are going through.
What is the answer?
What can they do?
What can I do?
Can I be a blessing?
Can I be a part of the hope they need?
What can I do?

One week. Seven days.
A smile gives a little.
It changes nothing about what they are going through.
We talk.
They share their story.
I share mine.
We exchange part of ourselves.
I don't have answers, only more questions.

What can they do to change what is happening?
What can I do to help?
Can I be a blessing?
Can I be a part of the hope they need?
Maybe I can't.
I can though do something because
I know the person who holds their hope and their future.
I know the person who knows the answer.
I touch their hand.
I share His love.
I share His joy that makes me smile.

They smile back and there I see it——

Hope.
Hope for today.
Hope for tomorrow.

Facets of the Father

You are many things, my Father.
Each of Your children know You
By their experience with You.
I know you too.
This I know to be true.

You are...

Truth when I am unsure.
Comfort when I cry.
Love when I am unlovable.
Hope when I am uncertain.
Strength when I am weak.
Mercy when I am unworthy.
Security when I am lost.
Wisdom when I am ignorant.
Peace when I am unsettled.
Life when I die.

You are many things, God, to many people.
The many things you are to me, Father,
Make me feel blessed to be Your child.
Thank you for being so much to me.

Just Ordinary

Jesus said "Follow Me".

What does that mean? Does He mean *me*?

Is He talking to *me*?

He must be talking to those who can do a lot for him.

He can't be talking to me. *I* can't go with Him.

I am just an ordinary person. Followers are *more* than ordinary.

They have something special about them. Something I don't have.

I have no gifts. What could *I do* for the Messiah?

I don't know much about the Bible.

I can't recall what God created on what day.

I don't know what sea Moses crossed.

I don't even know the names of the disciples.

I do believe in doing good things, but what Jesus asks,

I just can't do.

He will ask me to give up too much. I am sure I couldn't do it.

However....

I would like to follow Someone who knows the way.

I would like to know that Someone loves me for who I am.

I would like to know that Someone will teach me the things I do not understand.

I would like to believe in something more than myself.

I would like to have Someone who knows all about me and cares for me anyway.

Oh, I do want to follow Jesus!

I want to be promised life eternal!

I can leave it all behind for Him.

But, surely Jesus wasn't talking to *me* when He said "Follow Me".

I am just an ordinary person.

Heaven's Child

The words of a child
Are so innocent and grand.
They speak in love and in joy
And on our hearts, their words will land.

Their thoughts are full of innocence
And their love is so pure.
They speak of what they know
And teach us of what they're sure.

Through our hearts and in our lives
They speak what is true.
Oh, what we have gained,
When we look in their eyes anew.

They giggle at things
That we often never see.
We forget what it means
To pretend, to love, and just to be.

The children are called.
They are called with Jesus to sit.
A place we long to be.
A place they can't wait to get.

They speak in eagerness and in love
And pray for their hearts' desire.
They listen for the words of Jesus,
Knowing that of them, He will never tire.

Oh, the thoughts of a child.
Their world is so bright.
As we gaze down at them,
Let us share in their light.

I remain confident of this: I will see the goodness of the LORD in the land of the living.
Wait for the LORD; be strong and take heart and wait for the LORD.
Psalm 27:13-14

For everything that was written in the past was written to teach us, so that through the endurance taught in the Scriptures and the encouragement they provide we might have hope.
Romans 15:4

In Six Days

To look at the height of the mountains
and view the depths of the sea,
I know that You, my Father in Heaven,
have created it just for me.

The promise of the rainbow,
You place after the rain.
Reminds me of how true You are
and how close to You I must remain.

Thank You, God, for the majesty of a mountain
and the cool summer breeze in June.
Each reminds me of how great You are
and how we will be together so very soon.

In the spring, You give me the flowers,
Each morning, You give me the sun.
Let me, each day, be thankful for these.
My Father, Your will be done.

To experience the splendor of a sunset
or delight in the songs of a child.
I know that You, my awesome God,
were once too, so tender and mild.

God, Creator of Heaven and Earth.
I look around at this world You made in awe.
You made it in all its' beauty,
I am so glad I hear Your call.

The call to You, O God.
The call that calls me to Your place.
To the place that is more beautiful than here.
O Father, how I long to see Your face.

Even though, this is not my home.
I thank You, for this place I reside.
For in its beauty, I see you.
And in You, Father, I abide.

Into the Light

How do I tell you what I know?
What will I say?
The angels are waiting to rejoice;
They are waiting to rejoice this very day.

An illness, you say?
Only darkness you see?
How do I tell you;
that He died for you and for me?

The places you've been;
the things you've done.
Only God can deliver you now
from the hold of Satan, the evil one.

Will you laugh at what I say?
Will you curse? Will you spit?
I must tell you about this Man who died.
I must tell you what He did.

You plea for help with tears in your eyes.
How do I tell you? What do I say?
Jesus loves you and laid down His life.
He wants to free you this very day.

I work up my courage;
to do what is right.
"My friend", I say "Jesus can help."
"He'll lift you from darkness into the light."

She did not laugh and did not curse.
She just looked at me and grinned.
"Tell me more", she said as she bowed her head
and prayed " for I have sinned."

My Essence

My soul cries out for you, Lord.

My heart longs for the love only You can give.

My mind craves the knowledge that can only come from Your Word.

God, I thirst for a cup of Living Water.

I am starving, Father, feed me the Bread of Life.

As I yearn for each breath of air, God, I yearn for You.

Take this old body and make it new again.

Oh God, how I long to be full of who You are.

A Mom's Heart

God formed him before I knew him.

God touched him before I held him.

God knew his name before I named him.

God loved him before I loved him.

That is why he is so special to me.

Because he is so special to God.

A gift from God.

A blessing from heaven above.

I was hardly qualified to be a mother.

But through God, I am made able.

I love him because he is part of me,

but mostly because he is part of God.

I am thankful to God for trusting him to me.

I will do my best to raise him the way he should go.

He is a kiss from the God who is ever present in my life.

If you declare with your mouth, "Jesus is Lord," and believe in your heart that God raised him from the dead, you will be saved.

Romans 10:9

Have I not commanded you? Be strong and courageous. Do not be afraid; do not be discouraged, for the LORD your God will be with you wherever you go.
Joshua 1:9

My Gift to You

Do not be brokenhearted;
For it is **joy** I give to you,
An anointing and gladness.
For I have made your heart anew.

Do not be lonely;
For I sent to you my **son**.
He loves you as much as I.
His life he gave for everyone.

Do not be frightened;
For it is **courage** that I give.
The boldness to love and to care,
The braveness of spirit to really live.

Do not be silent;
For I give to you my **Word**;
Through the spirit your mouth may speak
Throughout the world the Truth be heard.

Do not be weak;
For what I give will make you **strong**.
The strength to stand, the strength to fight;
when all is against you and says you are wrong.

Do not be captive;
From bondage you have been set free
Live as if you are boundless,
Live as I have called you to be.

Dad

I thank you Dad, for letting me see the real you.

Thank you Dad, for letting me know it is okay to cry.

Thank you for being the Dad that I have waited a long time to know.

I appreciate knowing that you love me.

I appreciate knowing that you are proud of me.

I know that you care for me.

Thank you for letting me remain your little girl in my heart.

I want you to know that I love you.

I love your sense of humor and your insight.

Thank you especially for bringing me to Sunday School and teaching me to change a flat tire.

These two things have saved me from a life of despair and knowing how to do something in case someone else does not.

Thanks you for changing your life and changing mine in the process.

You are a wonderful father to whom I will always look up to.

GOODBYE, MY FRIEND

OH, THE LAUGHS, THE TEARS,

THE SHARING OF STRUGGLES AND TRIUMPHS,

THE PRAYERS FOR EACH OTHER AND FOR STRANGERS,

THE ENCOURAGING, THE PRAISING, AND THE STORIES WE'VE TOLD.

ONE WOULD THINK WE HAD BEEN FRIENDS FOR AGES.

IN GOD WE HAVE, FOR HIS TIME IS DIFFERENT THAN OUR OWN.

WHETHER WE HAVE SHARED FOR DAYS OR FOR YEARS,

THAT IS NOT WHAT MAKES A FRIEND.

IT IS THE HEART THAT MAKES A FRIEND.

THE OUTSIDE WILL FADE AWAY.

BUT THE HEART HOLDS ON TO THE TRUTH, AS OUR HEARTS DO.

FOR NOW, I SAY GOOD-BYE, MY FRIEND,

KNOWING THAT WE WILL SEE EACH OTHER AGAIN.

I THANK GOD FOR MAKING YOU MY SISTER.

AND I THANK HIM FOR GIVING US THE HEART TO MAKE US FRIENDS.

MY ROCK

HE IS MY STRENGTH.

HE IS MY ROCK.

I CAN STAND FIRM ON WHO HE IS.

THE ROCK STANDS FIRM

THOUGH THE WATERS RUSH BY.

THE ROCK STANDS FIRM

THOUGH THE RAIN COMES DOWN.

THE ROCK STANDS FIRM

THOUGH THE WINDS BLOW HARD.

NOTHING.

NO, NOT ANYTHING CAN

MOVE MY ROCK.

HE IS MY STRENGTH.

HE IS MY ROCK.

I CAN STAND FIRM ON WHO HE IS.

Ask, and it will be given to you; seek, and you will find; knock, and it will be opened to you. For everyone who asks receives, and the one who seeks finds, and to the one who knocks it will be opened.   Matthew 7:7-9

And the peace of God, which transcends all understanding,
will guard your hearts and your minds in Christ Jesus.
Phillipians 4:7

One Day

One day, I doubted, God.
I doubted what You gave me.
I couldn't hear You through the noise.

One day, I doubted, God.
I doubted that I had a gift.
I couldn't see You through the fog.

One day, I doubted, God.
I doubted that You could trust me.
I had forgotten You chose me.

One day, I doubted, God.
And on this day, I say I am sorry.

I know You love me.
I know and understand what You gave me.
Forgive me, my Lord, for sometimes, I forget.
Sometimes, I just can't hear You through
the noise and fog of this world.

Oh, thank You, Father.
That through my doubts, You are still there.
And through those doubts, You still love me.

RUNNING THE RACE

ACROSS THE FINISH LINE, YOU WAIT.
YOU WAIT TO CATCH ME IN YOUR ARMS.

YOU HAVE WAITED A LONG TIME.
I WILL SOON BE THERE.

YOU WAIT TO CATCH ME WITH THE SAME ARMS
THAT HELD ME BEFORE I WAS BORN.

YOU WANT TO SHOW ME THE PLACE YOU HAVE PREPARED.
THE PLACE THAT I HAVE BEEN RUNNING TO FIND.

WHILE I HAVE BEEN RUNNING,
YOU HAVE BEEN RUNNING BESIDE ME, HOLDING MY HAND.

WHILE I HAVE BEEN RUNNING,
YOU HAVE BEEN RUNNING BEHIND ME, GIVING ME STRENGTH.

WHILE I HAVE BEEN RUNNING,
YOU HAVE BEEN RUNNING IN FRONT OF ME, SHOWING ME THE WAY.

YOU NOW WAIT ACROSS THE FINISH LINE TO CATCH ME IN YOUR ARMS.

The Faithful Shepherd

I am Your sheep.
You are my Shepherd.
I follow Your voice because I know it.
You guide me right with Your staff.
Thank You, my Shepherd,
for guiding me, so that I can make it
to the place You have prepared for me.

My Shepherd, at times, I think that I know a better way.
I follow a different path that may look smooth.
What I find is that I am lost.
As a sheep, I am scared and frightened
because I know I don't know my way.
I know I will starve on my own.
I cry the tears of sorrow,
for I know I was wrong.
As I wipe my tears, I look up.
There You are.
You, too wipe Your tears.
Yours though are tears of joy.
For You are happy because You found me.
I know You are happy.
You left the rest of the flock to find me.

Thank You, my Good Shepherd.
For without You, I would surely die.

This Light

One dark night, in a place surrounded by few,
a small child was born.
He wasn't any child, of course.
He was the Messiah.
The one that generations had waited for.
The one that had been talked about long before His time.
He was the one that would save the world.
Many wondered how. Many thought they knew.
Many did not even care. But many did.
The way the child entered this world
was not with trumpets or horns.
Not with parties or champagne.
Few knew what great meaning this birth meant.
Though it was one dark night in a stable,
a light was present.
This light was brighter than any star.
Even brighter than the star that guided the distant strangers.
This light was brighter than any star and brighter than any sun.
This light was more than a light.
This light had just been born.
His name was Jesus. He was the Light.
Today, He is still the Light.
Let this Light forever shine!

And forever shine shall He!

God made two great lights—the greater light to govern the day and the lesser light to
govern the night. He also made the stars.

Genesis 1:16

Therefore, if anyone is in Christ, the new creation has come:
The old has gone, the new is here!
2 Corinthians 5:17

Holes

All through this life, I have gotten holes in my soul.
Some were caused by others and some caused by myself.
Some were just caused from living in this world.
But through all that, God, You can heal me.
As long as I let You.

You knew the holes in me as they were being made.
People laughed at me and a hole was made.
Since I turned it inward, the hole grew bigger.
People rejected me and another hole began to form.
Since I sought the world's acceptance, that hole grew deeper.
People hated me and yet another hole was made.
Since, I pursued the love of man, that hole too, grew wider.

God, I tried to fix those holes by myself, in my own way.
It did not work. The holes just kept growing.
And even more were made.
I worked and worked very hard to patch them up.
For years I tried different ways, but to no avail.
Then, I finally gave them to You.
I gave them to You, my Lord God Almighty, and they were healed.

It was hard, God, to give them up.
They were holes that I had for a very long time.
I know you were waiting for me to realize
that You are the only One that can take the tattered and make it whole.

I fall back sometimes to my old ways. To those same old holes.
Trying to fix those holes myself.
It never works, no matter how many times I try.
I am comforted when I turn and You are there, waiting,
not just to fix my holes, but to make me new again.

You say, You have been here all along.
Waiting for me to tire.
Waiting for me to turn to You.
Waiting for me to ask You to make me whole again.

You are the only One who can fix my holes.
Regardless of the years I have carried them.
Regardless of who caused them.
Regardless of how big or small.
and regardless of how deep or shallow.

You are the Healer, God and You are the Counselor.
I must listen when You say that you have what I need.
Then I must give You the holes that I've held so long.
But, You always let me choose: I can continue to live with my
holes or I can let You, who created me,
make me new once more.

Thank you, God, for doing just that.

Therefore we do not lose heart. Though outwardly we are wasting away,
yet inwardly we are being renewed day by day.
2 Corinthians 4:16

If you declare with your mouth, "Jesus is Lord," and believe in your heart that God raised him from the dead, you will be saved.

Romans 10:9

The Lord is my strength and my defense; he has become my salvation.
He is my God, and I will praise him, my father's God, and I will exalt him.
Exodus 15:2

And without faith it is impossible to please God, because anyone who comes to him must believe that he exists and that he rewards those who earnestly seek him.
Hebrews 11:6

Because

Follow me, not because others do,
but because you want a changed life.

Pray to me, not because you have to,
but because it is an honor and privilege to do so.

Serve me, not because it feels good,
but because I made you.

Believe me, not because it is right for the occasion,
but because my words are true and will never fail.

Give to me, not because I need anything,
but because others do.

Honor me, not because I demand it,
but because I am holy, just, and deserving.

Obey me, not because it keeps you out of trouble,
but because it shows me that you love me.

Seek me, not because everything else is empty,
but because I am the only thing that will complete
you.

Sing to me, not because you sound great,
but because it is a testimony of me.

Ask of me, not because you deserve it,
but because my grace is sufficient and I want to bless
you.

Go deeper with me, not because people will be
impressed,
but because that is a desire for both of us.

Trust me, not because you have nothing left to trust,
but because I always fulfill my promises.

Love me, not because you are good at it,
but because I first loved you.

And if I go and prepare a place for you,
I will come back and take you to be with me that you also may be where I am.
John 14:3

Be joyful in hope, patient in affliction, faithful in prayer.
Romans 12:12

As a deer pants for flowing streams, so pants my soul for you, O God.
My soul thirsts for God, for the living God.
Psalm 42:1

But seek first his kingdom and his righteousness, and all these things will be given to you as well. Therefore do not worry about tomorrow, for tomorrow will worry about itself. Each day has enough trouble of its own. Matthew 6:33-34

Then I saw "a new heaven and a new earth," for the first heaven and the first earth had passed away, and there was no longer any sea.
Revelation 21:1

Acknowledgments

To my family and friends for their constant encouragement of my ongoing endeavors! You mean so much to me. I thank God for you all!

Thank you especially to my husband, Glen, who pushes me higher and still keeps me grounded.

Most importantly, I am thankful to my Lord Jesus Christ, who is my everything.

For what is our hope, our joy, or the crown in which we will glory in the presence of our Lord Jesus when he comes? Is it not you? Indeed, you are our glory and joy.
I Thessalonians 1:19-20

Printed in the USA
CPSIA information can be obtained
at www.ICGtesting.com
LVHW071947011123
762649LV00019B/782